WHY OPOSSUM IS GRAY

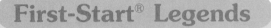

First-Start® Legends

WHY OPOSSUM IS GRAY

A STORY FROM MEXICO

Retold by Janet Palazzo-Craig
Illustrated by Charles Reasoner

Troll

Long ago, there was a little opossum. No one paid much attention to her, especially not Iguana. For only Iguana knew how to make fire, and he was very proud.

One night, Opossum heard Iguana talking. "I am the Great Firemaker! I should rule the village. I will run away and take my fire with me. Then all will see how important I am." Off he ran.

The next day, the village was in an uproar. "Without fire, we cannot cook! Without fire, we will freeze!" the villagers said. Opossum tried to speak, but no one would listen.

Finally, Opossum spoke again. "I saw Iguana take the fire up to the sky," she said.

At first, the villagers did not believe her. Then Raven said, "I will go see." Spreading his wings, he flew away.

At last, Raven returned. "Opossum was right," he said. "Iguana has taken the fire up to where the mountain meets the sky.

"We must find someone who can climb. Someone who is clever and quick. Someone who can bring the fire back!"

Everyone looked at Opossum. She was a good climber. "Will you help us?" they asked.

"Why should I?" said Opossum. "Before this, you never listened to me."

Then she saw how they shivered. She felt her own warm, white coat. "All right," said Opossum. "I will try."

Opossum set off. She climbed and climbed. The wind blew. The air was cold. Yet on and on she climbed.

Finally, she reached the top. There sat Iguana before a fire. "May I warm myself by your fire?" said Opossum.

"No," said Iguana. "You will take it!"

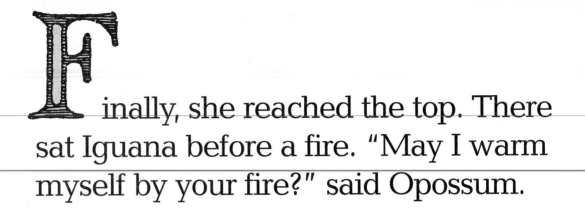

"Surely one as great and wise as you can guard your fire from me," said the little opossum.

"You are right," said Iguana. And he began to talk of how very great he was.

As Iguana talked, Opossum secretly curled her tail around a stick in the fire. The fire was hot, but she held on to it.

Would Iguana never look away?

At last, Iguana closed his eyes.

Opossum saw her chance! Away she ran, the burning stick held tightly in her tail. Behind her ran the angry Iguana.

At the edge of the mountain, Opossum threw the stick. Down to the village it fell.

"Thief!" cried Iguana angrily. He
threw a stick. It hit Opossum.
Opossum thought quickly. She
curled into a ball and did not move.

"Are you dead?" asked Iguana.
He poked at her, and she rolled
down the mountain.

From below, the villagers saw her falling. Raven flew up, using his wings to catch her.

The villagers wrapped her in a blanket. "Is brave Opossum dead?" they cried.

Opossum opened her eyes. "No, I am not!"

The villagers cheered. "Opossum, you are brave, quick, and clever!"

Iguana had been fooled. He stamped his feet. Then he ran away and hid among the rocks.

In time, the villagers learned how to make fire. As for Opossum, she still has the marks of the fire—a smoky gray coat and a black, hairless tail. If you see her, she may pretend to be dead. It is an old trick that has served her well!

Why Opossum Is Gray is a folktale from the Cora Indians, who are found in the mountains of Mexico. The ancestors of the Cora Indians are believed to be the mighty Aztecs.

This legend is an example of a trickster tale. In such tales, a weaker creature outsmarts a powerful enemy. Trickster heroes from other cultures include Ananse the Spider from Africa and Coyote from the American Southwest.

Mexican iguana